D0126114

The 7 Habits of
Highly Effective Teens:

THE MINIATURE
EDITION™

The
7 HABITS
of Highly Effective
TEENS:
THE MINIATURE EDITION™

The Ultimate Teenage Success Guide

by SEAN COVEY

RUNNING PRESS
PHILADELPHIA · LONDON

A Running Press® Miniature Edition™
© 2002 by Sean Covey
All rights reserved. Used under authorization. All rights reserved under the Pan-American and International Copyright Conventions

Printed in China

Library of Congress Cataloging-in-Publication Number: 2002108896

ISBN 978-0-7624-1474-1

This book may be ordered by mail from the publisher.
Please include $1.00 for postage and handling.
But try your bookstore first!

Running Press Book Publishers
2300 Chestnut Street
Philadelphia, Pennsylvania 19103-4371

Visit us on the web!
www.runningpress.com

CONTENTS

Get in the
the
Habit

They
Make You
or
Break
You

Welcome! My name is Sean and I wrote this book. I don't know how you got it. Maybe your mom gave it to you to shape you up. Or maybe you bought it with your own money because the title caught your eye. Regardless of how it landed in your hands, I'm really glad it did. Now you just need to read it. If you promise to read this book, I promise to make it an adventure. In fact, to make it fun, I've stuffed it full of cartoons, clever ideas, great quotes, and incredible stories about teens.

This book is based on another book that my dad, Stephen R. Covey, wrote several years ago entitled *The 7 Habits of Highly Effective People*. Surprisingly, that book became one of the all time best-selling books. He owes a lot of credit for its success to me, and my brothers and sisters, however. You see, we were his guinea pigs. He tried out all of his psycho experiments on us, and that's why my brothers and sisters have major emotional problems (just kidding, siblings). Luckily, I escaped uninjured.

So why did I write this book? I wrote it because life for teens is no longer a playground. If I've done my job right, this book can help you navigate through it. Unlike my dad's book, which was written for older people (and can really get boring at times), this book was written especially for teens and is always interesting.

I suspect that some of the struggles that teens have shared with me are also familiar to you:

"How can I feel good about myself when I don't match up? Everywhere I look I am reminded that someone else is smarter, or prettier, or more popular. I can't help but think, 'If I only had her hair, her clothes, her personality, her boyfriend, then I'd be happy.'"

"I feel as if my life is **out** of control."

"My family is a disaster. If I could only get my parents off my back I might be able to live my life. It seems that they are constantly nagging me, and I can't ever seem to satisfy them."

"I'm not doing too well in school right now. If I don't get my grades up, I'll never get into college."

The problems are real, and you can't turn off real life. Instead I will give you a set of tools to help you deal with real life. There are seven habits, that happy and successful teens have in common.

Habit 1: Be Proactive
Take responsibility for your life.

Habit 2: Begin with the End in Mind
Define your mission and goals in life.

Habit 3: Put First Things First
Prioritize, and do the most important things first.

Habit 4: Think Win-Win
Have an everyone-can-win attitude.

**Habit 5: Seek First to Understand,
Then to Be Understood**
Listen to people sincerely.

Habit 6: Synergize
Work together to achieve more.

Habit 7: Sharpen the Saw
Renew yourself regularly.

One great way to understand what the 7 Habits are is to understand what they are not. So here are the opposites, or:

THE 7 HABITS OF HIGHLY DEFECTIVE TEENS

Habit 1: React

Blame all of your problems on your parents, your stupid teachers, or professors, your lousy neighborhood, your boy- or girlfriend, the government, or something or somebody else. Be a victim. Take no responsibility for your life. Act like an animal. If you're hungry, eat. If someone yells at you, yell back. If you feel like doing something you know is wrong, just do it.

Habit 2: Begin with No End in Mind

Don't have a plan. Avoid goals at all costs. And never think about tomorrow. Why worry about the consequences of your actions? Live for the moment. Sleep around, get wasted, and party on, for tomorrow we die.

Habit 3: Put First Things Last.

Whatever is most important in your life, don't do it until you have spent sufficient time watching reruns, talking endlessly on the phone, surfing the Net and lounging around. Always put off your homework until tomorrow. Make sure the things that don't matter always come before those that do.

Habit 4: Think Win-Lose.

See life as a vicious competition.

Your classmate is out to get you,
so you'd better get him or her first.
Don't let anyone else succeed at
anything because, remember, if
they win, you lose. If it looks like
you're going to lose, however, make
sure you drag that sucker down
with you.

Habit 5: Seek to Talk First, then Pretend to Listen.

You were born with a mouth, so
use it. Make sure you talk a lot.

Always express your side of the story first. Once you're sure everyone understands your views, then pretend to listen by nodding and saying "Uh-huh." Or if you really want their opinion, give it to them.

Habit 6: **Don't Cooperate.**

Let's face it, other people are weird because they're different from you. So why try to get along with them? Teamwork is for the dogs. Since you

always have the best ideas, you are
better off doing everything yourself.
Be your own island.

Habit 7: **Wear Yourself Out.**

Be so busy with life that you never
take time to renew or improve
yourself. Never study. Don't learn
anything new. Avoid exercise like
the plague. And for heaven's
sake, stay away from good books,
nature, or anything else that may
inspire you.

As you can see, the habits listed
above are recipes for disaster.
Yet many of us indulge in them
regularly. And given this, it is no
wonder that life can really stink
at times.

WHAT EXACTLY ARE HABITS?

Habits are things we do repeatedly.
But most of the time we are hardly
aware that we have them. They're
on autopilot.

Some habits are good, such as:
- Exercising regularly
- Planning ahead
- Showing respect for others

Some are bad, like
- Thinking negatively
- Feeling inferior
- Blaming others

Depending upon what they are, our habits will either make us or break us. We become what we repeatedly do. As writer Samuel Smiles put it:

Sow a thought,
and you reap an act;

Sow an act,
and you reap a habit;

Sow a habit,
and you reap a character;

Sow a character,
and you reap a destiny.

Luckily, you are stronger than
your habits. Therefore, you can
change them. For example, try folding your arms. Now try folding them

in the opposite way. How does this feel? Pretty strange, doesn't it? But if you folded them in the opposite way for thirty days in a row, it wouldn't feel so strange. You wouldn't even have to think about it. You'd get in the habit.

At any time you can look yourself in the mirror and say, "Hey I don't like that about myself," and you can exchange a bad habit for a better one. It's not always easy, but it is possible.

Building Your Personal Bank Account

Before you'll ever win in the public arenas of your life, you must first win the private battles with yourself. All change begins with you. I will never forget how I learned this lesson.

"What's wrong with you? You're disappointing me. Where's the Sean I once knew in high school?" Coach glared at me. "Do you ever want to be out there?"

I was shocked. "Yes, of course."

"Oh, just give me a break. You're just going through the motions and your heart's not in it. You better get your act together or the younger quarterbacks will pass you up and you'll never play here."

It was my sophomore year at Brigham Young University (BYU) during preseason football camp. Coming out of high school, I was recruited by several colleges but chose BYU because they had a tradition of producing all-American quarterbacks like Jim McMahon and Steve Young, both of whom went on to the pros and led their teams to Super Bowl victories. Although I was the third-string quarterback at the time, I wanted to be the next all-American!

When Coach told me I was "stinkin' up the field," it came as a cold, hard slap in the face. The thing that really bugged me is he was right. Even though I was spending long hours practicing, I wasn't truly committed. I was holding back and I knew it.

I had a hard decision to make—either I had to quit football or triple my commitment. Over the next several weeks, I waged a war inside my head and came face to face with many fears and self-doubts. Did I have what it takes to be the starting quarterback? Could I handle the pressure? Was I big enough? It soon became clear to me that I was scared, scared of competing, scared of being in the limelight, scared of trying and perhaps, failing. And all of these fears were holding me back from giving it my all.

I read a great quote by Arnold Bennett that describes what I finally decided to do about my dilemma. He wrote, "the real tragedy is the tragedy of the man who never in his life braces himself for his one supreme effort—he never stretches to his full capacity, never stands up to his full stature."

Having never enjoyed tragedy, I decided to brace myself for one supreme effort. So I committed to

giving my all. I decided to stop holding
back and to lay it all on the line. I did
know if I would ever get the chance to
be first string, but if I didn't, at least I
was going to strike out, swinging.

No one ever heard me say, "I com
mit." There was no applause. There
was simply a private battle I fought
and won inside my own mind over a
period of several weeks.

Once I committed myself, everything changed. I began taking chanc
and making big improvements on th

field. My heart was in it. And my coach took notice.

As the season began and the games rolled by one by one, I sat on the bench. Although frustrated, I kept working hard and improving.

Midseason featured the big game of the year. We were to play nationally ranked Air Force on ESPN, in front of 65,000 fans. A week before the game, Coach called me into his office and said I would be the starting quarterback. Gulp! Needless to say, that was the longest week of my life.

Game day finally arrived. At kickoff, my mouth was so dry, I could barely talk. But after a few minutes I settled down and led our team to victory. I was even named the ESPN Player of the Game. Afterward, lots of people congratulated me on the victory and my performance. But they didn't really understand.

They didn't know the real story. They thought the victory had taken place on the field that day in the public eye. But I knew it happened months before in the privacy of my own head, when I decided to face my fears, to stop holding back, to brace myself for one supreme effort. Beating Air Force was a much easier challenge than overcoming myself. Private victories always come before public victories. As the saying goes, "We have met the enemy and he is us."

How you feel about yourself is like a bank account. Let's call it your *personal bank account* (PBA). Just like a checking or savings account at a bank, you can make deposits or withdrawals from your PBA by the things you think, say and do. For example, when I stick to a commitment I've made myself, I feel in control. It's a deposit. On the other hand, when I break a promise to myself, I feel disappointed and make a withdrawal.

So let me ask you: How is your PBA? How much trust and confidence do you have in yourself? Are you loaded or bankrupt?

If your personal bank account is low, don't get discouraged. Just start today by making $1, $5, $10 or $25 deposits. Eventually, you'll get your confidence back. Small deposits over a long period of time is the way to a healthy and rich PBA.

With the help of various teen groups, I've compiled a list of six key deposits that can help build your PBA. Of course, with every deposit, there is an equal and opposite withdrawal.

PBA DEPOSITS

Keep promises to yourself

Do small acts of kindness

Be gentle with yourself

Be honest

Renew yourself

Tap into your talents

PBA WITHDRAWALS

Break personal promises

Keep to yourself

Beat yourself up

Be dishonest

Wear yourself out

Neglect your talents

Basically, there are two **kinds** of people in this world—the **proactive** and the reactive—those **who** take responsibility for their live**s, and** those who blame; those **who** make it happen, and those who **get** happened to.

Each day you and I ha**ve** about 100 chances to choose whe**ther** to be proactive or reactive. **In any** given day, the weather is **bad,** you can't find a job, you lose a**n election** at school, you get a par**king ticket**

on campus, you flunk **a** test. So
what are you going to **do** about it?
Are you in the habit **of** reacting to
these everyday kinds **of** things, or are
you proactive? The **cho**ice is yours.
It really is.

Reactive people **make** choices
based on impulse. **They** are like a
can of soda pop. If life **sh**akes them
up a bit, the pressure **buil**ds and they
explode: Hey, you **stupid** jerk! Get
out of my lane!

Proactive people **make** choices

based on values. They think before they act. They recognize they can't control everything that happens to them, but they can control what they do about it. Unlike reactive people who are full of carbonation, proactive people are like water. Shake them up all you want, take off the lid, and nothing. No fizzing, no bubbling, no pressure. They are calm, cool, and in control.

"I'm not going to let the other guy get me upset and ruin my day."

You can usually hear the difference between proactive and reactive people by the type of language they use. Reactive language usually sounds like this:

"That's me. That's just the way I am." What they're really saying is, "I'm not responsible for the way I act. I can't change. I was predetermined to be this way."

Or: "Thanks a lot. You just ruined my day." What they're really saying is, "I'm not in control of my own moods."

Notice that reactive language takes power away from you and gives it to something or someone else. As my friend John Bytheway explains in his book, *What I Wish I Had Known in High School*, when you're reactive, it's like giving someone else the remote control to your life and saying, "Here, change my mood anytime you wish." Proactive language, on the other hand, puts the remote control back in your own hands.

Proactive people are a different breed. Proactive people:

- Are not easily offended
- Take responsibility for their choices
- Think before they act
- Bounce back when something bad happens
- Always find a way to make it happen
- Focus on things they can do something about, and don't worry about things they can't

Being proactive usually means
two things. First, you take responsibility for your life. Second, you
have a "can-do" attitude. Can-do is
very different from "no-can-do."
Just take a peek.

If you think can-do, and you're
creative and persistent, it's amazing
what you can accomplish. During
college, I remember being told that
to fulfill my language requirement I
would "have to" take a class that I
had no interest in and was meaning-

less to me. Instead of taking this class, however, I decided to create my own. I put together a list of books I would read and assignments I would do and found a teacher to sponsor me. I then went to the dean of the school and presented my case. He bought into my idea and I completed my language requirement by taking my self-built course.

American aviator Elinor Smith once said, "It has long since come to my attention that people of accomplishment rarely sit back and let things happen to them. They went out and happened to things."

It's so true. To reach your goals in life, you must seize the initiative. If you're feeling bad about not being asked out on dates, don't just sit around sulking about it. Find ways to meet people. Be friendly. Try smiling a lot. Ask them out. They may not know how great you are. Similarly, don't wait for the perfect job to fall into your lap, go after it. Send out your resume, network, volunteer to work for free.

Dermell Reed once told me how his proactive response to a family crisis changed his life forever. His 13-year-old brother had been shot and killed in a drive-by shooting. One muggy August night, a few weeks after Kevin's death, Dermell got a hold of .38 caliber revolver and went out in the streets to get revenge on the crack dealer who had killed his brother. He was within

fifty feet of the man, when he paused
and caught hold of himself. He used
his imagination to think about what
he wanted to make out of his life. He
listened to his conscience, and knew
that if he took revenge, he'd be
throwing away his future.

Using raw willpower, Dermell,
instead of giving in to his anger
and throwing away his life, got up,
walked home and vowed that he
would finish college for his dead
brother. Nine months later, Reed

made the honor roll and graduated from high school. People in his school couldn't believe it. Five years later, Reed became a college football star and a college graduate.

Like Dermell, each of us will face an extraordinary challenge along the way, and we can choose whether to rise to those challenges or be conquered by them. Elaine Maxwell sums up the entire matter quite well. "Whether I fail or succeed shall be no man's doing but my own. I am the force. I can clear any obstacle before me or I can be lost in the maze. My choice: my responsibility; win or lose, only I hold the key to my destiny."

So let me ask you: are you in the driver's seat in your life or are you merely a passenger?

Control **Your** **Destiny** or **Someone** **Else** **Will**

You draw up a blueprint before you build a house. You read a recipe before you bake a cake. In the same way, you choose who you want to become so you can actively make that happen.

Let me show you how to do that using your imagination. Find a place where you can be alone without interruption. Now clear your mind of everything. Don't worry about school, friends, family, or that zit on your forehead. Just focus with me,

breathe deeply, and open your mind.
In your mind's eye, visualize someone walking toward you about a
half-block away. As this person gets
closer and closer, you suddenly real-
ize, believe it or not, that it's you.
But it's not you today. *It's you as you
would like to be one year from now.*

Now think deeply.

What have you done with your
life over the past year?

How do you feel inside? What
characteristics do you possess?

(Remember, this is you as you would
like to be one year from now.)

You can float back to reality now.
If you were a good sport and actually
tried this experiment, you probably
got in touch with your deeper self.
You got a feel for what's important
to you and what you'd like to accomplish this next year. That's called
beginning with the end in mind.
And it doesn't even hurt. In fact,
thinking beyond today can be really
quite exciting.

Why is this so important? I'll give you two reasons. The first is that you are at a critical crossroads in life, and the paths you choose now can affect you forever. The second is that if you don't decide your own future, someone else will do it for you.

So if it is so important, how do you do it? The best way I have found is to write a personal mission statement. A personal mission statement is like a personal credo or motto that states what your life is about. They come in all types and varieties. Some are long and some are short. Some teens have used their favorite quote as a mission statement. Others have used a picture or a photograph.

A personal mission statement is like a tree with deep roots. It is stable and isn't going anywhere, but is also alive and constantly growing. You need a tree with deep roots to help you survive all of the storms of life that beat you up. As you've probably noticed already, life is anything but stable. Think about it. People are fickle. Your boyfriend loves you one minute and dumps you the next. You're someone's best friend one day, and they're talking behind your back the next.

Think about all the events you can't control. You have to move. You lose your job. Your parents are getting divorced.

While everything about you changes, a personal mission statement can be your deep-rooted tree that never moves. You can deal with change if you have an immovable trunk to hang onto.

THE GREAT DISCOVERY

The Great Discovery is a fun activity designed to help you get in touch with your deepest self as you prepare to write a mission statement. Answer the questions honestly. When you're finished, I think you'll have a much better idea of what inspires you, what you enjoy doing, whom you admire, and where you want to take your life.

1. Think of a person who made a positive difference in your life. What qualities does that person have that you would like to develop?

2. Imagine 20 years from now, when you are now surrounded by the most important people in your life. Who

are they and what are you doing?

---

3. If a steel beam were placed across two skyscrapers, for what would you be willing to cross? A thousand dollars? A million? Your pet? Your brother? Fame? Think carefully.

---

4. List 10 things you love to do. It could be singing, dancing, looking at magazines, drawing, reading,

daydreaming . . . anything you absolutely love to do!

5. Five years from now, your local paper does a story about you and they want to interview three people: a parent, a brother and sister, and a friend. What would you want them to say about you?

6. Think of something that represents you . . . a rose, a song, an animal.

Why does it represent you?

7. If you could spend an hour with any person who ever lived, who would that be? Why that person? What would you ask?

8. Everyone has one or more talents. Which in the following list are you good at? You can also write down ones that are not listed:

Good with numbers

Good with words

Creative thinking

Athletics

Making things happen

Sensing needs

Artistic

Working well with people

Decision making

Accepting others

Speaking

Writing

Dancing

Listening

Singing

Humorous

Sharing

Music

Now that you've taken the time to walk through The Great Discovery, you've got a good jumpstart on developing a mission statement. You're not writing it for your English teacher and it's not going to be graded by anyone. It is your secret document. So make it sing! The most important question to ask yourself is, "Does it inspire me?" If you can answer yes, you did it right!

Organize
for
Success

Have you ever packed a suitcase and noticed how much more you can fit inside when you neatly fold and organize your clothes instead of just throwing them in? The same goes for your life. The better you organize yourself, the more you'll be able to pack in—more time for family and friends, more time for school, more time for yourself, more time for your first things.

PLAN WEEKLY
Take fifteen minutes each week to

plan your week and just watch what a difference it can make. Why weekly? Because we think in weeks and because daily planning is too narrow a focus, and monthly planning is too broad a focus. Once you have a planner of some sort, follow this three-step weekly planning process:

Step 1: Identify Your Big Rocks

At the beginning or end of each week, sit down and think about what you want to accomplish for the upcoming week. Ask yourself, "What are the most important things I need to do this week?" I call these your big rocks. They are sort of like mini-goals and should be tied to your mission statement and longer-term goals. You might come up with the list of big rocks that looks something like this:

My Big Rocks for the Week:

- Study for a science test
- Finish reading a book

- Attend Megan's game
- Complete employment application
- Party at Isabella's
- Exercise 3 times

Another way to identify your big rocks is to think through the key roles of your life, such as your role as a student, friend, family member, worker, individual, and whatever else you do, and then come up with the one or two most important things you want to get done in each role. Planning your life around your roles will help you stay balanced.

Step 2. Block Out Time for Your Big Rocks

Have you ever seen the big rock experiment? You've got a bucket and fill it half full of small pebbles. You then try to put several big rocks in the bucket, on top of the pebbles. But they don't all fit. So you empty the bucket and start over. This time you put the big rocks in first,

followed by the pebbles. This time,
it all fits. Big rocks represent your
most important things. Pebbles
represent all the little everyday
things that suck up your time, such
as chores, busy work, phone calls,
and interruptions.

During your weekly planning
sessions, block in time for your
big rocks by booking them in your
planner. For example, you might
decide that the best time to get
started on your history final is

Tuesday night and the best time to call your grandma is Sunday afternoon. It's like making a reservation.

Step 3. Schedule Everything Else

Once you have your big rocks booked, schedule in all of your other little to-dos, daily tasks, and appointments. Here's where the pebbles go. You might also want to look ahead on your calendar and

record upcoming events and
activities, like a vacation, concert,
or birthday.

THE COMMON INGREDIENT
OF SUCCESS

In the final analysis, putting first
things first takes discipline. It takes
discipline to manage your time. It
takes discipline to overcome your
fears. It takes discipline to be strong
in the hard moments and resist peer
pressure. A man named Albert E.

Gray, who spent years studying
successful people, concluded that:

*"All successful people
have the habit of doing the things
failures don't like to do.
They don't like doing them neces-
sarily either. But their disliking
is subordinated to the strength
of their purpose."*

The Key to Communication

It's our tendency to want to swoop out of the sky like Superman and solve everyone's problems before we even understand what the problem is. We simply don't listen. The key to communication and having power and influence with people can be summed up in one sentence. If you can learn to see things from another's point of view before sharing your own, a whole new world of understanding will be opened up to you.

Why is this the key to communication? It's because the deepest need of the human heart is to be understood. Everyone wants to be respected and valued for who they are. "People don't care how much you know until they know how much you care." How true it is.

FIVE POOR LISTENING STYLES

To understand someone you must listen to them. Surprise! The problem is that most of us don't know how to listen. When people talk we seldom listen because we're usually too busy preparing a response, judging, or filtering their words through our own paradigms. It's so typical of us to use one of these five poor listening styles:

Spacing out is when someone is talking to us but we ignore them because our mind is wandering off in another galaxy. They may have something important to say, but we're caught up in our own thoughts.

Pretend listening is more common. We still aren't paying much attention to the other person, but at least we pretend we are by making insightful comments at key junctures, such as "yeah," or "cool." The speaker will usually get the hint and will feel that he or she is not important enough to be heard.

Selective listening is where we pay attention to the part of the conversation that interests us. Since you'll always talk about what you want to talk about, chances are you'll never develop lasting friendships.

Word listening occurs when we actually pay attention to what someone is saying, but we listen only to the words, not to the body language, the feelings, or the true meaning behind the words. As a result we might miss what's really being said.

Self-centered listening happens

when we see everything from our own point of view. Instead of standing in another's shoes, we want them to stand in ours "You think your day was bad? That's nothin'. You should hear what happened to me."

Judging. Sometimes, as we listen to others, we make judgements (in the back of our minds) about them and what they're saying. People don't want to be judged, they want to be heard.

GENUINE LISTENING

Luckily, you and I never exhibit any of these five poor listening styles. Right? Well, maybe occasionally. There is a higher form of listening. We call it "genuine listening." And it's the kind of practice we want to put to use.

First, listen with your eyes, heart, and ears. Listening with just your ears isn't good enough, because only 7 percent of communication is contained in the words we use. The rest comes from body language and how we say words.

To hear what other people are saying, you need to listen to what they are not saying. No matter how hard people may appear on the surface, most everyone has a tender inside and has a desperate need to be understood.

Second, stand in their shoes. To become a genuine listener, you need to take your shoes off and stand in another's shoes. In the words of Robert Bryne, "Until you walk in another man's moccasins you can't imagine the smell." You must try and see the world as they see it and try to feel as they feel.

Third, practice mirroring. Think like a mirror. It doesn't judge. It doesn't give advice. It reflects. Mirroring is simply this: Repeat back in your own words what the other person is saying and feeling. Mirroring isn't mimicking. Mimicking is when you repeat exactly what the other person says, like a parrot.

Balance Is Better

How you do in one dimension of life will affect the other three. If one of your car's tires is out of balance, all four tires will wear unevenly, not just the one. It's hard to be friendly (heart) when you're exhausted (body). It also works the other way. When you're feeling motivated and in tune with yourself (soul), it's easier to focus on your studies and to be more friendly (heart).

TAKE TIME FOR A TIME OUT

Just like a car, you need regular tune-ups and oil changes. You need time out to rejuvenate the best thing you've got going for yourself—you! You need time to relax, unstring your bow, treat yourself to a little tender loving care. So let's look at each of the dimensions and specific ways to sharpen the saw:

CARING FOR YOUR BODY

Your body is a tool, and if you take

good care of it, it will serve you well.
Here is a list of 10 ways teens can
keep themselves physically sharp:

Eat good food

Relax in the bathtub

Bike

Lift weights

Get enough sleep

Practice yoga

Play sports

Take walks

Stretch out

Do an aerobic workout

There's much truth to the
expression, "You are what you eat."
I'm not an expert in nutrition but
I have found two rules of thumb to
keep in mind. First, listen to your
body. Pay careful attention to
how different foods make you feel
and from that, develop your own
handful of do's and don'ts. Everyone
responds differently to food. For
example, whenever I eat a big meal
right before bed I feel horrible in the
morning. And whenever I eat too

many french fries, nachos, or pizza, I get a "grease rush." (Have you ever had one of those?) These are my *don't*s. On the other hand, I've learned that eating lots of fruits and vegetables and drinking tons of water makes me feel sharp. These are my *do's*.

Second rule of thumb. Be moderate and avoid extremes. For many of us (me included), it's easier to be extreme than moderate, and so we find ourselves jumping back and forth between eating a rabbit-food and junk-food diet. But extreme eating habits can be unhealthy. A little junk food on occasion isn't going to hurt you. Just don't make it your everyday fare.

The USDA food pyramid is a balanced and moderate approach to nutrition that I highly recommend. It encourages eating more whole grains, fruits, vegetables, and low-fat dairy products and eating less fast food, junk food, and snacks, which are often loaded with fat, sugar, salt, and other gook. Remember, food affects mood, so eat with care.

Speaking of mood, we all feel depressed, confused, or apathetic at times. And it's at times like these when perhaps the best thing we can do for ourselves is do what Forrest Gump did: exercise ourselves better. Besides being good for your heart and lungs, exercise has an amazing way of giving you a shot of energy, melting stress away and clearing your mind.

Just be careful. In your quest for a better physique, make sure you don't become too obsessed with your appearance. Before you start comparing yourself to the babes and hunks on the cover of *Cosmopolitan* or *Muscle and Fitness* and begin hating everything about your looks, please remember that there are thousands of healthy and happy teens who don't have high cheekbones, rock-hard ABs, or buns of steel. And even the so-called beautiful people aren't perfect.

Many years ago, actress Michelle Pfeiffer was featured on the front cover of *Esquire* magazine with the caption, "What Michelle Pfeiffer needs. . . . is absolutely nothing." But she actually needed more help than meets the eye. *Harper's* had obtained the photo retoucher's bill for Pfeiffer's picture on the *Esquire* cover. The retoucher charged $1,525 to render the following services: "Clean up the complexion, soften smile line, trim chin, soften line under earlobe, add hair, add forehead to create better line and soften neck muscles." The editor of *Harper's* printed the story because we are, he said, "constantly faced with perfection in magazines; this is to remind the reader . . . there's a difference between real life and art."

CARING FOR YOUR BRAIN

Try to develop your brainpower through your schooling, extracurricular activities, hobbies, jobs, and other mind-enlarging experiences. Perhaps more than anything else, what you do with that mass of gray material between your ears will determine your future. Unless you want to be flipping burgers and living with your parents when you are thirty years old, you'd better start paying the price now.

I'd suggest you get as much education as you can. Any further education beyond high school—

a college degree, vocational or technical training, an apprenticeship, or training in any of the armed forces—will be well worth your time and money. See it as an investment in your future. Statistics have shown that a college graduate earns about twice as much as a high school graduate.

CARING FOR YOUR HEART

The heart is a very temperamental thing. And it needs constant nourishment and care, just like your body. The best way to sharpen the saw is to make regular deposits into your own personal bank account, which I explained earlier, and your "relationship bank account." Here's how to do that:

"Relationship Bank Account" (RBA) Deposits

- Keep promises
- Do small acts of kindness
- Be loyal

- Listen
- Say you're sorry
- Set clear expectations

"Personal Bank Account" (PBA) Deposits

- Keep promises to yourself
- Do small acts of kindness
- Be gentle with yourself
- Be honest
- Renew yourself
- Tap into your talents

As you might have noticed, PBA
and RBA deposits are very similar.
That's because deposits you
make into other people's accounts
usually end up in your own as well.
I like how Mother Teresa put it:
"Let no one come to you without
ever leaving better and happier.
Be the living expression of God's
kindness: kindness in your face,
kindness in your eyes, kindness in
your smile." If you approach life
in this way, always looking to

build instead of tear down, you'll
be amazed at how much happiness
you can give to others and find
for yourself.

CARING FOR YOUR SOUL

What is it that moves your soul?
By soul, I mean that inner self that
lurks far below the surface of your
everyday self. Your soul is your cen-
ter, wherein lies your deepest
convictions and values. It is the
source of purpose, meaning and

inner peace. Sharpening the saw in the spiritual area of life means taking time to renew and awaken that inner self. As the famous author Pearl S. Buck wrote, "Inside myself is a place where I live alone and that's where you renew your springs that never dry up."

Here are a few ways teens say they feed their soul:

- Meditating
- Serving others

- Writing in a journal
- Going for a walk
- Reading inspiring books
- Drawing
- Praying
- Writing poetry or music
- Thinking deeply
- Listening to uplifting music
- Playing a musical instrument
- Practicing a religion
- Talking to friends
- Reflecting on personal goals or mission statement

In summary, self-renewal won't just happen to you. Since it's an important but not urgent activity, you have to be proactive and make it happen. The best thing to do is to take out time each day for these life-balance activities, even if it's only for fifteen or thirty minutes. Some teens set aside a specific time each day—early in the morning, or after school or late at night—to be alone, to think to exercise. There's no one right way—so find what works for you.

Well, this is the end of the book. Thank you for journeying with me and congratulations on finishing. I just want to let you know that I truly believe in your future. You were destined for great things. Always remember, you were born with everything you need to succeed! You don't have to look anywhere else! The power and light is in you!

Before signing off, I'd like to

leave you with a favorite quote of mine, by Bob Moawad. I wish you all the best.

You can't make footprints in the sands of time by sitting on your butt! And who wants to leave buttprints in the sands of time?

This book has been bound
using handcraft methods and Smyth-
sewn to ensure durability.

The dust jacket is based on one designed
by Barry Litmann.

The cover and interior was designed
by Frances J. Soo Ping Chow.

The text was edited by
Deborah Grandinetti and Annie Oswald.

The text was set in Goudy, Gill Sans
and Times New Roman.

For additional FranklinCovey books,
products and other services, please visit
www.franklincovey.com.